LUDWIG VAN BEETHOVEN

SCENA AND ARIA

'Ah, Perfido!'
for Soprano and Orchester
Op. 65

Edited by/Herausgegeben von
Max Unger

T0081306

Ernst Eulenburg Ltd

London · Mainz · Madrid · New York · Paris · Tokyo · Toronto · Zürich

L. VAN BEETHOVEN

Scena and Aria
'Ah, perfido!'

Beethoven composed 'Ah, perfido' in 1795/96, soon after his Piano Trios Op. 1 had appeared in print. Hoffmeister and Kühnel eventually published this early work without opus number. Tobias Haslinger referred to it as '46. Werk' in 1832, though it had already been listed as Op. 65 by Artaria in 1819. This confusion was caused by using unclaimed opus numbers to close the gaps in the chronological order of Beethoven's compositions.

'Ah, perfido' dates from the period when Beethoven was studying the treatment of the voice and the setting of Italian texts with Salieri. The work is, however, much more than a mere exercise. The expression is comparable to that of the great arias in *Fidelio*, and the formal construction is completely convincing, in spite of the frequent changes of mood and tempo. The orchestration is individual in its colouring because the woodwind section has no oboes. The instrumental sound is therefore unusually mellow and provides a perfect background for the eloquent wind solos which comment on the Italian text no less passionately than the voice itself. The soprano part is dramatic and exacting. Its range covers two octaves up to the high B flat.

It appears from a sketchbook in the British Museum that Beethoven began the composition in Vienna. He must have finished it during a visit to Prague in February 1796 because he wrote on the cover of a score which had been copied by someone unknown (but corrected by Beethoven himself): 'Une grande Scène mise en Musique par L. v. Beethoven à Prague 1796.' He also inscribed the following dedication on the first page of the same score: 'Recitativo e Aria composta e dedicata alla Signora di Clari di L. v. Beethoven.' This score has been lost, as well as the greater part of the autograph. Only two sheets (four pages) of the original manuscript score have been preserved, and these are now in the library of the Paris Conservatoire. Though Countess Josephine von Clary was praised for her singing in the *Jahrbuch der Tonkunst für Wien und Prag* (Vienna, 1796), the first performance was apparently given by Josepha Duschek on the 21 November 1796 in Leipzig. Beethoven also included the work in his subscription concert (*Akademie*) on the 22 December 1808, in which the Fifth and Sixth Symphonies and the Choral Fantasy, Op. 80, were performed for the first time.

'Ah, perfido' was published in 1805 by Hoffmeister and Kühnel for voice and piano, together with the orchestral parts. Schott reprinted the parts in 1811, but no full score was published until 1856 (by Peters). The present Eulenburg edition was prepared by Max Unger before the Last War. His sources were the parts published by Schott, as well as the Peters full score which is largely based on the same parts.

The Italian text of the opening (pp. 1-7), is from *Achille in Sciro*, an opera libretto by Metastasio; the author of the remainder is unknown. The German translation printed in this Eulenburg score was first published by André in a vocal score. The name of the translator has not been recorded.

The gist of the rather dramatic text is as follows: *Scena:* The soprano (Deidamia) curses the unfaithful traitor (Achilles) who leaves her, but she changes her mind (Adagio) and would rather die for him since she still loves him. *Aria:* She pleads with her idol not to leave her, but he is evidently unrepentent, because she accuses him of cruelty (Allegro assai) and asks— the audience presumably—whether she does not deserve to be pitied.

Stefan de Haan, 1971

L. VAN BEETHOVEN

Szene und Arie

„Ah, perfido!"

Beethoven komponierte „Ah, perfido" in den Jahren 1795/96, also bald nach der Veröffentlichung seiner Klaviertrios Op. 1. Als Hoffmeister und Kühnel dieses frühe Werk schliesslich herausgaben, erschien es ohne Opusnummer. Noch 1832 bezeichnete Tobias Haslinger es als „46. Werk", obgleich es schon 1819 in einer Liste Artarias als Op. 65 angeführt worden war. Diese konfuse Nummerierung war dadurch entstanden, dass man Opusnummern, die noch ohne Werke geblieben waren, dazu benutzte, um die Lücken in der chronologischen Reihenfolge von Beethovens Werken zu schliessen.

„Ah, perfido" stammt aus der Zeit, in der Beethoven die Behandlung der Stimme und das Vertonen italienischer Texte studierte, doch ist das Werk viel bedeutender als eine gewöhnliche Kompositionsübung. Der Ausdruck lässt sich mit dem der grossen Fidelioarien vergleichen, und die musikalische Form wirkt, trotz häufiger Stimmungs- und Tempowechsel, durchaus überzeugend. Die Instrumentierung ist in der Tonfarbe für Beethoven ungewöhnlich, weil unter den Holzbläsern keine Oboen sind. Der Orchesterklang ist daher besonders schmelzend und wird so zur idealen Begleitung für die Soli der Bläser, die den italienischen Text nicht weniger leidenschaftlich untermalen als die Stimme selbst. Die Sopranstimme ist dramatischen Charakters und stellt an die Sängerin hohe Anforderungen. Ihr Umfang erstreckt sich über zwei Oktaven bis zum hohen B.

Ein Skizzenbuch, das sich im British Museum befindet, beweist, dass Beethoven die Komposition in Wien angefangen hat. Er muss sie aber im Februar 1796 in Prag vollendet haben, denn er schrieb auf den Umschlag einer von unbekannter Hand kopierten (aber von Beethoven verbesserten) Partitur: „Une grande Scène mise en Musique par L. v. Beethoven à Prague 1796." Ausserdem schrieb er die folgende Widmung auf die erste Seite derselben Partitur: „Recitativo e Aria composta e dedicata alla Signora di Clari di L. v. Beethoven." Diese Partitur und der grösste Teil des Autographs sind heute unauffindbar. Nur zwei Blätter (vier Seiten) der von Beethoven eigenhändig geschriebenen Originalpartitur haben sich erhalten, und diese befinden sich zur Zeit in der Bibliothek des Pariser Konservatoriums. Obwohl Gräfin Josephine von Clary als Sängerin im *Jahrbuch der Tonkunst für Wien und Prag* (Wien, 1796) gerühmt wurde, war es nicht sie, sondern Josepha Duschek, welche das Werk bei seiner vermutlichen Erstaufführung in Leipzig am 21. November 1796 vortrug. Es wurde auch in Beethovens *Akademie* am 22. Dezember 1808 aufgeführt, in der seine fünfte und sechste Sinfonie, sowie die Chorphantasie Op. 80, zum ersten Mal gespielt wurden.

„Ah, perfido" wurde 1805 von Hoffmeister und Kühnel im Klavierauszug, zugleich aber auch mit den Orchesterstimmen, veröffentlicht. Schott brachte 1811 einen Neudruck der Stimmen heraus, aber die Partitur erschien erst 1856 bei Peters. Die vorliegende Eulenburg-Partitur wurde vor dem letzten Krieg von Max Unger herausgegeben. Als Quelle benutzte er die von Schott verlegten Stimmen, sowie die Partitur von Peters, die grösstenteils auf den erwähnten Orchesterstimmen beruht.

Der italienische Text des ersten Teils (S. 1-7) ist aus Metastasios Libretto *Achille in Sciro*, doch der Autor des zweiten Teils ist unbekannt. Die in der vorliegenden Eulenburg-Partitur gedruckte deutsche Übersetzung erschien erstmalig in einem von André herausgebrachten Klavierauszug ohne Nennung des Übersetzers.

Stefan de Haan, 1971

Scena and Aria

'Ah, perfido!'

L. van Beethoven Op. 65
1770-1827

2.

Andante quasi Adagio

Fl.

Clar. in B

Fag.

Cor. in Es

Vl. I.

Vl. II.

Vla.

Sopr.
par - ti?
las - sen?

Vlc.
e Basso

Fl.

Clar. in B

Fag.

Cor. in Es

Vl. I.

Vl. II.

Vla.

Sopr.
e son que - sti gl'ul - ti - mi tuoi con - ge - di?
und sind dies dei - ne letzten Ab-schieds-wor - te?

O - ve s'in-te - se ti - ran - ni - a più cru -
O gibt es wohl ein Herz so kalt und hart wie

Vlc.
e Basso

E. E. 4843

Aria
Adagio

per lui vi - ve - a, voglio mo - rir per lu - i!
für ihn nur lebt' ich, ich will für ihn auch sterben!

E. E. 4843

14

Fl.

Clar. in B

Fag.

Cor. in Es

Vl. I.

Vl. II.

Vla.

Sopr.

bar - ba-ra mer - cè.   si   bar - ba-ra mer - cè?   Di-te voi.se in   tan-to af-
To - des-qual zum Lohn, ach To - des-qual zum Lohn? Sa-get, fühlt ihr nicht Er -

Vlc.
e Basso

Fl.

Clar. in B

Fag.

Cor. in Es

Vl. I.

Vl. II.

Vla.

Sopr.

fan-no non son   de- gna di pie - tà.   non son de-gna di pie - tà,· non son
bar-men für   dies tief ge - kränkte   Herz?   sa-get, fühlt ihr nicht Er - barmen, für dies

Vlc.
e Basso

18

E. E. 4843

24

ta?
Herz?